Secret M

Philosophy In Crayon

Carole Johnston

abuddhapress@yahoo.com

ISBN: 9798867391539

Most of these poems were published in *Atlas*

Poetic-a Tanka Journal 2015 and *Hedgerow A Journal of Small Poems 2015*

crayons

like Eliot's Cats

need new names

not just Crayola names

I write their secret colors

I want all

those green and gold boxes

on the shelf

inhale the scent of rainbow

my fingers touch each hue

I pull

out crayons one by one

sniff them

roll each around my hands

choose "Big Sky" and "Zen Poem"

with her

"Wind In The Blossoms"

crayon

April writes a poem

to the grass

it's a redbud riot

"Wild Rumpus" crayon

hooligan spring

cracks a dragon egg

inside me

april is

a jade green dragon

crayon named

"Meander" she wanders

a buttercup sky

spring city

a "Circus of Cerise"

scarlet crayon

"Razzmatazz Sequins"

and "Sunny Day Jazz"

children write

poems about the taste

of yellow

the "Sun Snoring"

crayons melting

"Purple Eyes"

morning glory violet ink

glass jar on my desk

fingers clutch crayons

and fountain pen

I grip

that "Bruise Blue" crayon

striking

thunder sky on the page

never neurotypical

I want to

smear "Swallowtail" crayon

all over

this rainy grey day

paint tangerine wings

blood moon

while we grumbled

in our sleep

she disappeared

"Penumbra" crayon

new crayon

twirling swirling siennas

tumbleweed

mixed with burnt umber

I call it "Song Sparrow"

I search

for the daffodil path

crayons

named "Pollen Dreams"

color it streetlight bright

"Gull's Voice"

is my "Sea Blue" crayon

when will I

live by the shore again

Buddha eyes on horizon

clutching my

"Sonic Silver" crayon

I float clouds

the color of thunder

explode white lightning

soetimes

you can't get enough

yellow

all the crayons in the world

can't "Light Up This Rain"

confusion

"Confetti" of crayons

scribbled

by a hopscotch child

inside my motley head

which one

is the haiku crayon

living

in color of the moment

"Thunder Blue" or "Lizard Green?"

a crayon called

"The Moon Bleeds Silver"

keeps me awake

trying to write the face

of a newborn child

in my book

I color new synapses

sparking words

inside the brains of poets

a crayon called "Mystery"

"Spring Burst"

"Dogwood Salmon"

street sketch

my cherry blossom crayons

fading shades of April

"African Mask Red"

juxtaposed with "Ivy Green"

on my back porch

cardinals nesting in the vines

a crayon's deep heart

drawing with

your "Tarot Card" crayon

call it "Vision"

clear as candle wax

stay away from the flame

stone white crayons

"Angel Dogwood Green"

"Holy River"

I drive through a memory

of gratitude and rain

in space between

sky blue and cerulean

silence

a crayon called "Nowhere Zen"

another one called "Bliss"

if I were a crayon

I would fly up like butterflies

right out of the box

sipping on sunflowers

call me "Mariposa"

the shock

of a thousand daffodils

my "Inner Wordsworth"

crayon wanders cloud lonely

through everyone's inner child

a crayon called

"Flame" lights up my mornings

"Woke Yellow"

sun streams through sparrowsong

the world spins and glows

Walt Whitman's

favorite electric crayons

"Neon Grass"

"Lincoln Lilacs Blooming"

and still more pain in April

"Rumbling Sludge"

crayon smudges the mountain's

coal black eye

colors for strip mining

"Appalachia's Pearly Tears"

Jersey Shore sunrise

all crayons in the box

can't capture it

my memories "Gull Blue"

and "Tangerine Joy"

Holy Land burning

 crayons called "Bombs Exploding"

"Flaming Sand"

colors of bleeding corpses

hues of horror and pain

in a sketch book

crayons called "Riots & Death"

broad waxy strokes

of "Smoke" and "Charred Ruins"

too much crimson and black

bruise on the city

a crayon called "Police Blue"

crushes the scene

"Midnight Riot" draws chaos

across neon billboards

"Dead Chipmunk"

soulful striped crayon

rusty earth

and burnt sienna

dark side of the sun

a crayon

called "Vincent at Arles"

infused with

sunflowers stars and wheat fields

touching it I feel the heat

Monet crayons

called "Impression Sun"

"Lumin Pink"

"Peonies At Dawn"

springlight us into May

faith is glass

a "Cobalt Blue" crayon

numinous

in the moonlit window

vaporizing before dawn

naming crayons

"Stained Glass" "Dream Mandala"

wax flowing down

a broken bottle in the dark

scratching hope

Facebook wants

to tell me the color

of my "soul" but

my "Essence- Blueluminous"

hides in the crayon box

pandemic crayon

"Green Glow In The Window"

each night I go to bed

with eerie intuition…something

creeps behind me… jaws open

a crayon called

"Grandmother Frog Pond"

"Moon Mother" "Goddess

of Green and Grey"

her head resting in clouds

whispers secrets to the sky

Carole Johnston, poet, novelist and retired Creative Writing Teacher, lives in Lexington, Kentucky. She has published 4 books of poetry: **Journey's: Getting Lost** - Finishing Line Press, **Manic Dawn** - Wildflower Poetry Press, **Purple Ink - A Childhood in Tanka** - Finishing Line Press, **Midnight Butterfly and Other Juxtapositions,** Alien Buddha Press. She has also published many Japanese short form poems in a large variety of journals.

Printed in Great Britain
by Amazon

37496813R10030